DISCARDED

The Transcontinental Railroad

by Jean F. Blashfield

Content Adviser: Professor Sherry L. Field,
Department of Social Science Education, College of Education,
The University of Georgia

Reading Adviser: Dr. Linda D. Labbo,
Department of Reading Education, College of Education,
The University of Georgia

COMPASS POINT BOOKS

Minneapolis, Minnesota

Compass Point Books
3722 West 50th Street, #115
Minneapolis, MN 55410

Visit Compass Point Books on the Internet at *www.compasspointbooks.com* or e-mail your request
to *custserv@compasspointbooks.com*

Editors: E. Russell Primm, Emily J. Dolbear, and Deborah Cannarella
Photo Researcher: Svetlana Zhurkina
Photo Selector: Linda S. Koutris
Designer: Bradfordesign, Inc.
Cartographer: XNR Productions, Inc.

Library of Congress Cataloging-in-Publication Data

Blashfield, Jean F.
    The transcontinental railroad / by Jean F. Blashfield.
        p. cm. — (We the people)
    Includes bibliographical references and index.
    ISBN 0-7565-0153-9
        1. Pacific railroads—Juvenile literature. [1. Pacific railroads. 2. Railroads—History.] I. Title.
II. We the people (Compass Point Books)
    TF25.P23 B53 2002
    385'.0979—dc21   2001001591

TABLE OF CONTENTS

WORK OF GIANTS

One of the great stories in American history is the building of the first railroad across the United States. Army General William T. Sherman called the project "a work of giants." The railroad ran from Omaha, Nebraska, to Sacramento, California—a distance of almost 1,800 miles (2,896 kilometers). It united the nation and made the United States one of the most powerful countries in the world.

When the idea of a **transcontinental** railroad was first proposed in 1838, many people laughed. At that time,

The trans-continental railroad near Green River, Wyoming

4

Many people traveling west in search of gold added to the need for a transcontinental railroad.

steam locomotives had been pulling cars on metal tracks for only ten years. Also, great natural barriers would have to be overcome in order to lay the track—obstacles such as the Mississippi River, the Rocky Mountains, and the rugged Sierra Nevada mountains.

As a result, the idea of building a railroad was forgotten—until the demand for one grew too great to ignore. During the **gold rush** of 1849, thousands of people traveled to California to hunt for gold and settle the region. The journey west was long and difficult. People soon realized that the country needed a transcontinental railroad.

SUPPORT AND BARRIERS

In 1848, railroads were being developed in the East, but most trains ran north and south. None traveled farther west than the Mississippi River. The first bridge across the river was built between Rock Island, Illinois, and Davenport, Iowa. It opened to rail traffic on April 22, 1856. When trains began to travel across the bridge, some steamboat

Abraham Lincoln

companies became afraid of losing business. Then a steamboat—perhaps accidentally and perhaps not—crashed into one of the bridge supports. The crash started a fire that destroyed all the wooden parts of the bridge.

The owners of the steamboat line refused to pay for the damage, however. They said the bridge was a danger to water travel. The Rock Island Bridge Company, which

6

The first bridge across the Mississippi River was between Rock Island and Davenport.

had built the bridge, took the matter to court. The company's lawyer was a young attorney named Abraham Lincoln. Eventually, Lincoln won the case. The U.S. Supreme Court decided that the steamboat company had no right to stop the railroad and had to pay for the damage to the bridge. Soon, new bridges were built across the Mississippi River. These bridges connected the small rail lines being built on each side of the river.

When President-elect Abraham Lincoln traveled from Illinois to Washington to be inaugurated in 1861, he made the entire trip by train. It took him twelve days to reach the White House, but he could have been there in two days. He spent extra time stopping along the way to meet the people of the country.

Even with bridges across the Mississippi River, people could not travel easily across the country. They could make the long trip from one coast to the other in three ways. Some settlers walked along the Oregon Trail, which **immigrants** had been traveling since the 1830s. This route covered 2,000 miles (3,218 km) and took six months.

Other people sailed to Central America and traveled across the **Isthmus** of Panama, a narrow strip of land that connects North and South America. This route passed through a jungle, and many travelers died of fever.

The third choice was to sail around the tip of South America. This trip took about six months and many ships were lost in those stormy seas.

In 1853, U.S. Secretary of War Jefferson Davis sent army engineers to find a land route for a transcontinental railroad. One of the biggest barriers the railroad would have to cross was the Sierra Nevada mountains, a steep and snowy range along most of California's eastern border. The engineers eventually found several possible routes for the railroad but, once again, the plan was postponed.

Arguments about the issue of slavery were then dividing the people of the Northern and Southern states. Southerners wanted the railroad to be built in the South. In fact, a southern route would have been the easiest route to build. The region has no large mountains and gets little snow. People in the northern states, however, knew that a southern railroad would strengthen the terrible institution

The Oregon Trail was one route.

9

William Sherman

of slavery. So the northern members of Congress refused to vote for a southern route, and the southern members refused to vote for a northern route.

In 1853, Captain William T. Sherman left the U.S. Army to start a company called the Sacramento Valley Railroad. By a stroke of luck, he met and hired a man called Theodore Dehone Judah. Judah had been born in Connecticut and worked as a railroad engineer in the East. People called him "Crazy Judah" because he talked about building a railroad west to California long before anyone else thought it was possible.

Sherman hired Judah to survey—measure and mark—the route east from Sacramento, California, into the foothills of the Sierra Nevada. The Sacramento Valley Railroad was completed in 1856.

Judah still dreamed of building a cross-country railroad. He traveled into the Sierra Nevada to find a route through the mountains. One day, he received a letter from Daniel W. Strong, a **druggist** who lived in the town of Dutch Flat. Strong told Judah about the old Donner Pass trail.

Theodore Judah

This route had been used by early settlers. In 1846, a group of settlers, who had set out too late in the winter season, starved to death while trapped there in heavy snows. Since that tragedy, the dangerous route had been abandoned and almost forgotten. Strong showed Judah the way through the Donner Pass. The men agreed that a train could travel through the Sierra Nevada along that trail.

Judah began trying to raise money to back the project. He traveled to Sacramento, California, where he held meetings at a hotel to explain his plan. There, he met four merchants—Leland Stanford, Charles Crocker, Mark Hopkins,

11

The men behind the transcontinental railroad

and Collis P. Huntington. These men, who were later known as the Big Four, decided to put up the money for the railroad. In June 1861, the Big Four formed the Central Pacific Railroad Company. Judah was named chief engineer. Less than three months later, Leland Stanford was elected governor of California.

At first, the Big Four funded the railroad by constructing the Dutch Flat and Donner Lake Wagon Road. The road served as a supply route for the materials needed to build the railroad. The company charged the miners and **merchants** a toll, or fee, to use the road. These tolls helped pay for the early months of work on the railroad.

During this time, Judah tried to convince the mem-

The site of the Dutch Flat and Donner Lake Road that would bring supplies to crews in the west

bers of Congress that the project should be funded by the federal government. By then, several southern states had **seceded**, or separated, from the Union. Northern lawmakers could now make their own decision about the best route for a cross-country railroad. President Lincoln had been a fan of railroads since 1831, when he wanted to start one in his home state of Illinois. On July 1, 1862, the president happily signed the Pacific Railroad Act.

Crazy Judah had succeeded. The government's help would now ensure that the railroad would finally be built. Sadly, however, Judah caught a fever while crossing the Isthmus of Panama and died in 1863. He never saw his dream come true.

TWO RAILROADS

The Pacific Railroad Act included a plan to get the work done quickly. The law said that two railroads would work toward each other until they met. The Union Pacific would lay track westward. It would eventually join the Central Pacific, which would lay track eastward.

Both railroad lines were given a lot of financial support. For every 1 mile (1.6 km) of track laid, each railroad company was given 6,400 acres (2,592 hectares) of land. Each company would also own the land on which the

tracks were built as well as any stations or other buildings on that land. This plan made the railroads the largest landowners west of the Mississippi— except for the U.S. government itself.

A Central Pacific passenger train arriving in Cisco

In return for building the railroad, each company received land grants.

Two years later, the Pacific Railroad Act was changed. Each railroad line would now receive twice as much land for every mile of track laid—12,800 acres (5,184 hectares). Other terms were also added to benefit the railroad companies and ensure that they would have enough money to finish the job. In the amended (changed) bill, President Lincoln also set a standard width for the tracks. America's railroad tracks would now have a "standard gauge" of 4 feet 8.5 inches (1.4 meters).

At first, the Union Pacific Railroad was controlled by large committees. Eventually, however, two men became the most important people behind the building of the westward-bound line.

Thomas Durant

Thomas Durant, called "Doc" Durant because of his medical training, was a New York businessman. Durant was in charge of managing the railroad's money. Unfortunately, he managed to put a lot of the money into his own pocket—but he also managed to get the railroad built.

The man in charge of the building of the railroad was Grenville Mellen Dodge. He was born in Massachusetts and trained as an engineer, but he also worked as a **surveyor**. A surveyor is a person who measures and records pieces of land. In 1859, Dodge had met Abraham Lincoln, who was elected president the next year.

Lincoln was making a speech in Council Bluffs, Iowa. When Lincoln

Grenville Mellen Dodge

16

heard that Dodge was an engineer, he wanted to meet him. The two men sat together until late in the night, talking about a transcontinental railway. They agreed that the railroad should start in Omaha, Nebraska, just across the Mississippi River from Council Bluffs.

Dodge was a general for the Union Army throughout the American Civil War (1861–1865). He built railroad lines to carry troops and supplies through the South and also repaired track damaged by the enemy. During his service under General Ulysses S. Grant, Dodge traveled west to St. Louis, Missouri. Grant, Dodge, and others feared that the Indians would prevent the railroad from being built across the Great Plains. The Indians were fighting to protect their hunting grounds and their homelands.

While battling the Indians, Dodge continued to look for the best routes for a railroad.

The war ended, and Dodge was released from active military service in 1866. He then took charge of the construction of the Union Pacific Railroad. The project was

17

behind schedule. The first track had been laid in 1865. The Union Pacific Railroad extended only 40 miles (64 km) by the end of that year. Dodge was ready to make the train thunder across the Plains.

The Central Pacific's first track had been laid in 1863 but by the summer of 1865, its line extended only 43 miles (69 km). The railway had reached the foothills of the Sierra Nevada mountains—one of the most difficult obstacles on the route. The company was running out of money, and expenses were growing. Also, the railroad did not have enough workers, and it was difficult to hire and keep men. Most men in California worked for themselves or preferred to work in mining. At one point, the Central Pacific had only 500 workers, although it needed thousands.

In 1865, Charles Crocker, one of the Big Four, heard about some

Charles Crocker

Chinese construction workers in the Sierra Nevada

Chinese workers who had helped build two small railroads in California. Some people believed that Chinese people were too small to do such hard labor. These workers had already proved themselves, however. And, as Crocker pointed out, "The Chinese made the Great Wall, didn't they?"

At first, as a trial, Central Pacific put only a few Chinese laborers on the payroll. When Crocker realized how skilled and reliable these workers were, he hired thousands more. Many already lived in California, but many others came from farms in China. By the end of the year, the Central Pacific had thousands of workers—and more than two-thirds of them were Chinese.

BUILDING TUNNELS

One of the greatest achievements of the Central Pacific Railroad workers were the tunnels they built through the Sierra Nevada. Between Cisco and Lake Ridge, for example, a distance of only 20 miles (32 km), they had to cut eleven tunnels.

The tunnels were cut by blasting rock out of the mountains. At that time, safety dynamite had not yet been invented. Blasting was a dangerous job. The workers used **black powder** to blast out the rock. For some of the tunnels, workers used about 500 kegs of black powder a day.

A Chinese worker leaving one of the railroad's many tunnels

20

On average, the laborers blasted out only about 6 to 12 inches (15 to 30 centimeters) of rock in a day. Later, some workers used liquid **nitroglycerin** instead. This explosive was about five times more powerful than black powder— and much more deadly.

The Chinese did most of the blasting. Many of them remembered how this dangerous work had been done in the mountainous regions of China. (Black powder was invented by the Chinese.) First, the workers were lowered down the steep mountain cliffs in baskets. They chipped holes in the rock with hammers and hand drills. Then they placed black powder in the holes and lit the fuse, rushing to get out of the way. Afterward, they removed the piles of broken rock in handcarts so that the work could continue.

To build the tunnel more quickly, teams of men worked at each end. Workers also cut into the middle of the mountain and worked toward the ends. Once the tunnels were completed, heavy rails were carted up the mountains to lay the track.

21

Deep snows in the mountains made work on the railroad very difficult.

The deep snows made winter very difficult and dangerous in the Sierra Nevada. Many men were killed in **avalanches**. The Chinese workers built tunnels under the snow so that they could keep working. Once the rock tunnel was cut, they could work inside the mountain. In the fall of the second year, they worked in three shifts, around the clock, to get inside the rock tunnel before the winter snows began.

As many as 8,000 men worked on the Sierra Nevada tunnels. The longest tunnel they built was the Summit Tunnel. It was 1,659 feet (506 m) long and lay 124 feet (38 m) below the surface. It took two years to complete the Summit Tunnel, and it was built at the highest elevation that the workers had reached—7,042 feet (2,148 m). On November 30, 1867, a Central Pacific locomotive pulled the first train from Sacramento through the Summit Tunnel. The Sierra Nevada mountains were no longer a barrier to the railroad's progress.

LIVING AND WORKING TOGETHER

At that time in California, Chinese people were often treated unfairly. The Chinese railroad workers on the Central Pacific Railroad were also treated badly at times. Some of the white railroad workers did not like working with them. But without the efforts of all of these men working together, regardless of their origins, the railroad could never have been built.

White and Chinese railroad workers lived quite differently from one another. White workers were paid about $30 a month. As part of their salary, they were also fed beef, beans, bread, butter, and potatoes. The Chinese earned about the same amount of money, but they had to buy their own food. They divided themselves into small groups, and each group had a cook. They ate a healthy diet of many different kinds of fish, vegetables, mushrooms, and fruit. They also drank hot tea—sometimes called

Many railroad workers lived together in tents.

"powder tea" because it was carried along the work routes in clean black-powder kegs.

All the men worked six days a week, from sunrise to sunset. At times, they even worked in shifts through the night. Sunday was their day off, and many spent their free time drinking and gambling. Most of the Chinese did not spend their money on entertainment, however. They saved their earnings to send to relatives in China or to buy them a ticket to America.

In warm weather, the Central Pacific Railroad workers lived in tents. Many of the Chinese laborers had come from farms. They were used to working outdoors and sharing crowded living areas. Six or more men slept comfortably in tents that measured only 10 by 12 feet (3 by 3.7 m).

During the final miles of railroad construction, Irish and Chinese laborers worked together.

The railroad workers who built the Union Pacific Railroad were known as "gandy dancers." They probably got this nickname because much of their equipment was made by the Gandy Company. They were also sometimes called the Irish laborers, to distinguish them from the Central Pacific's Chinese laborers. In addition to the Irish workers, however, the Union Pacific employed many former soldiers. These men had served in the American Civil War, in both the Confederate and Union armies.

The railroad also employed freed slaves and immigrants from many countries. The Union Pacific also hired

American Indians who lived on the land through which the railroad was being built. The railroad owners hoped that the Indians' tribes would then allow the railroad to pass through their lands.

The Union Pacific's laborers ate and slept in railroad cars. They sat at long tables where about 200 men could eat at one time. About 150 men slept in each car on bunk beds that were three tiers high.

Whole towns traveled with the men as they moved across the Great Plains. These towns came to be called "Hells on Wheels." The townspeople were saloonkeepers who sold the railroad workers alcohol, gamblers who were

Entire towns traveled with the construction workers.

glad to help the men get rid of their hard-earned money, and women who provided entertainment. When the workers started laying track beyond the town, the townspeople simply packed up and moved farther west with them. Often, the only trace they left behind was a small cemetery—the burial place of men who had been killed in accidents, in fights, or by American Indians.

Passing over mountains and plains, building a railroad was a gigantic task. It required thousands of workers and the careful timing of many different jobs.

The surveyors began the work. They chose and marked the route that the railroad would travel. They

Surveyors working on the Central Pacific portion of the railroad

searched for the straightest route possible. A road can easily be made to curve around a hill or a rocky area, but a curved railroad track cannot be built as easily. Surveyors also looked for a route that was near a body of water, because the locomotives were powered by steam.

The surveyors tried to find areas where material blasted out of a high spot could be used to fill in a low spot. If a low spot could not be filled, complicated frameworks had to be built to make a permanent platform. Each of these frameworks, called a trestle, had to be custom made for the site where it would go.

Behind the surveyors came the graders. These men worked with shovels, wheelbarrows, picks, and plows. They broke up the ground, removing all plant life from the path of the tracks. They also built a strong roadbed, or grade, on which the rails would be placed. The roadbed had to be above the ground so that rainwater would drain away from the tracks. It also had to be perfectly level. Some graders checked the level by eye. Others drove a

Graders worked to make the land level for the laying of the tracks.

team of oxen that pulled a board across the roadbed. The board scraped the surface level. The graders moved tons of rock every day for years. They had no machines, trucks, or bulldozers to help them. All the work was done with horses, oxen, wheelbarrows, and strong arms.

The men who laid the track worked about 100 miles (161 km) behind the graders. Their horses pulled wagons loaded with heavy iron rails and spikes. Each rail was 28 feet (8.5 m) long and weighed about 600 pounds (272 kilograms). The workers—usually five "iron men" to one rail—pulled the rails, one by one, from the wagon. At the signal—"Down!"—they positioned the rail on the railbed. The men worked together like machines. They could place four rails every minute. Another worker, called a gauger, measured the distance between the rails to be sure they were the correct distance apart. When the wagon was empty, the men pushed it off the track so that the next wagon could move up.

As the iron men positioned each rail, men working behind them drove iron spikes to attach the rails to the railbed. They put about ten spikes in each rail, striking each spike three times with a **sledgehammer**. Other men then attached nuts and bolts to the heavy bars that connected the two rails.

At every stage, bosses oversaw the work. Some directed the work of a small group. Others supervised entire work shifts. At the top were the construction

Laying the rails was a backbreaking and exhausting process.

31

managers, who worked directly for the railroad owners in Sacramento and New York.

John S. "Jack" Casement and his brother, Dan, managed the construction teams of the Union Pacific Railroad. James Harvey Strobridge was construction manager for the Central Pacific. Strobridge arranged to have his wife live with him on the construction train. The couple turned the railway car into a three-bedroom home and raised six children there. Strobridge's wife, Hanna Maria, even had a pet canary that traveled with them. Hanna Strobridge was probably the only woman to witness the entire construction of the railroad.

James Harvey Strobridge lived with his wife in a railroad car.

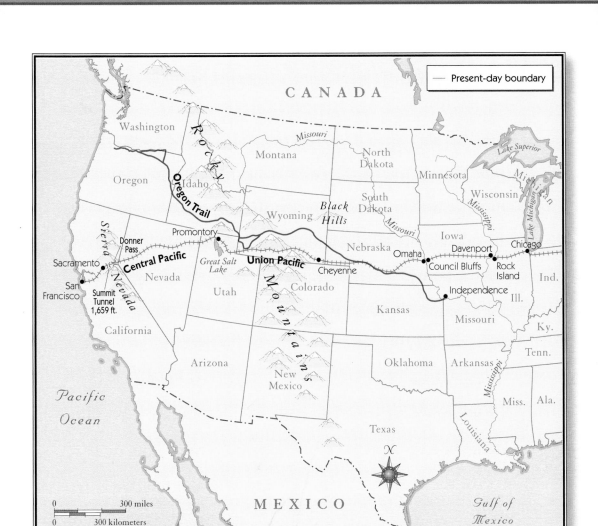

The route of the transcontinental railroad across the western United States

THE RACE IS ON

The Pacific Railroad Act did not indicate the point in the United States where the two railroad lines would meet. The Union Pacific railroad had the right to build as far as it could. The Central Pacific, however, did not have that same right. But each company was being paid for every mile of track it laid, so this arrangement was unfair to the Central Pacific Railroad.

In 1866, while the Union Pacific was already chugging across the Great Plains, the Central Pacific was still working on the tunnels of the Sierra Nevada. The managers of the Central Pacific went to Washington, D.C., to sort this out. They demanded the same rights as the Union Pacific Railroad—to cover as much ground as possible. That summer, Congress amended the Pacific Railroad Act again, to allow the Central Pacific to lay more track.

The race was on. The public was gripped by the contest. Reporters came from all over to follow the workers'

Mormon workers helped speed construction of the tracks across Utah.

progress and report the news to the nation.

In the spring of 1868, surveyors for the Union Pacific entered Utah. Doc Durant, the railroad's financial manager, wanted to hire more workers. He decided to ask Brigham Young for help. Young was the head of the Mormon Church that had settled Utah. He had also been one of the early investors in the railroad, so he agreed. Many Mormon farmers were glad to have outside work at that time because grasshoppers were destroying their crops. These strong, young workers speeded the Union Pacific's progress across Utah.

Meanwhile, the Central Pacific had finally come down from the mountains and entered Utah. The two lines were now getting closer to each other. Each day, news of their progress was sent by telegraph to the headquarters

35

of each railroad company. Workers were encouraged to work even faster. Soon, the lines were so close that graders for the two railroads were preparing railbeds right next to each other—each heading in the opposite direction and each pretending the other wasn't there!

The public didn't always hear about the nasty things that went on during this race to the finish. Sometimes, at night, workers on one railroad would wreck the work their competitors had done during the day. Sometimes men and animals were murdered.

The bitter competition did not stop until the government declared that the official meeting point of the rail-

Promontory, Utah, was the official meeting place for the tracks of the two companies.

Finally, the two companies met, joining the East Coast to the West Coast of the United States.

hammer and drove the spike in.

The Golden Spike was not really made of gold, of course. It was made of steel. This last spike completed the railroad, but it also completed the electrical circuit in the telegraph line built alongside the railroad. As Dodge drove in the spike, a telegraph signal was sent around the world—"D-O-N-E." The greatest engineering project of the nineteenth century was finished.

39

That telegraph signal launched thousands of celebrations across the United States. Parades began, and church bells rang. Cannons were fired in small towns everywhere, the first heard since the Civil War had ended four years earlier. The Eighth Wonder of the World had been built, and America had done it.

The ability to travel—and, because of the telegraph, to communicate—across the country brought the states closer together. The end of the Civil War had begun the

A. J. Russell photographed officials from the two railroads shaking hands.

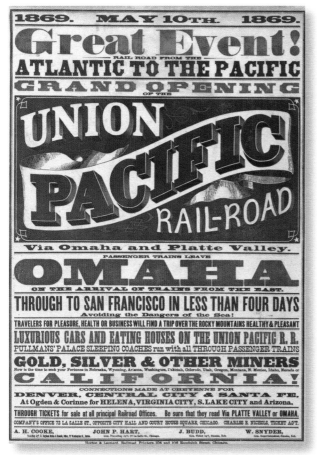

An ad for travel from Omaha, Nebraska, to San Francisco, California

process of joining America north and south. The new railroad joined the country east and west. The cross-country trip that took the early settlers six months to make could now be made in six days.

It took six years to make Crazy Judah's dream a reality. It also took the vision and leadership of many great men and the hard labor of some 20,000 others. Even though the railroad no longer exists, it was one of America's greatest achievements—truly the "work of giants."

GLOSSARY

avalanches—large masses of snow or rock that suddenly move down a mountain

black powder—a mixture of chemicals used in gunpowder, fireworks, and blasting

druggist—a person who sells medicines; a pharmacist

gold rush—the sudden arrival of crowds of people in search of gold

immigrants—people who leave one area to live in another

isthmus—a narrow strip of land connecting two larger areas of land

merchants—people who buy and sell goods

nitroglycerin—an explosive liquid used in making dynamite

seceded—withdrew from a group

sledgehammer—a large, heavy hammer with a long handle

surveyor—someone who measures areas of land for builders or mapmakers

transcontinental—crossing a continent

DID YOU KNOW?

- The Central Pacific workers had to blast out fifteen tunnels so that the railroad could travel through California's Sierra Nevada mountains.

- The only mechanical power used to build the transcontinental railroad was one steam shovel.

- On the last day of the race, Central Pacific workers laid track at the rate of almost 1 mile (1.6 km) per hour. In twelve hours, eight men laid 3,520 rails. Each man lifted about 125 tons of iron!

- When the railroad was finished, workers had laid about 700,000 rails and had hammered in about 7 million spikes— all by hand.

- After the railroad was completed the cross-country trip that took early settlers six months could be made in six days by train.

IMPORTANT DATES

Timeline

1838 — The idea of a transcontinental railroad is first proposed.

1862 — President Abraham Lincoln signs the Pacific Railroad Act on July 1.

1863 — The first rail of the Central Pacific Railroad is laid in Sacramento, California, on January 8.

1865 — The first rail of the Union Pacific Railroad is laid in Omaha, Nebraska. The Central Pacific begins to cross the Sierra Nevada mountains.

1866 — A fierce race to the finish begins between the two railroads.

1869 — The Central Pacific and Union Pacific railroads meet on May 10 at Promontory Summit, Utah, for the Golden Spike ceremony. The transcontinental railroad is completed.

IMPORTANT PEOPLE

CHARLES CROCKER
(1822–1888), *head of construction on the Central Pacific Railroad*

GRENVILLE MELLEN DODGE
(1831–1916), *chief engineer of the Union Pacific Railroad*

THOMAS "DOC" DURANT
(1820-1885), *financial manager of the Union Pacific Railroad*

THEODORE DEHONE JUDAH, OR "CRAZY JUDAH"
(1826–1863), *chief engineer of the Central Pacific Railroad*

ABRAHAM LINCOLN
(1809–1865), *sixteenth president of the United States*

WILLIAM T. SHERMAN
(1820–1891), *founder of the Sacramento Valley Railroad*

LELAND STANFORD
(1824–1893), *president of the Central Pacific Railroad, governor of California, and founder of Stanford University*

WANT TO KNOW MORE?

At the Library

Anderson, Peter. *The Transcontinental Railroad.* Danbury, Conn.: Children's
　　Press, 1996.

Fraser, Mary Ann. *Ten Mile Day: And the Building of the Transcontinental
　　Railroad.* New York: Henry Holt and Company, 1996.

Gregory, Kristiana. *The Great Railroad Race: The Diary of Libby West.* New
　　York: Scholastic, 1999.

Young, Robert. *The Transcontinental Railroad: America at Its Best?*
　　Englewood Cliffs, N.J.: Silver Burdett, 1996.

On the Web

Central Pacific Railroad Photographic History Museum

http://www.cprr.org/

Features photographs of the building of the Central Pacific railroad and
provides links to first-person accounts, articles from magazines of the period,
and related railroad, photography, and history sites

Golden Spike National Historic Site

http://www.nps.gov/gosp/home.html

Official site of the national park located at the spot where the Golden Spike
ceremony was held in 1869

Union Pacific Railroad Photo Gallery

http://www.uprr.com/aboutup/photos/

To view hundreds of images of the construction of the Union Pacific Railroad

Through the Mail

National Railroad Museum

2285 South Broadway St.

Green Bay, WI 54304

920/437-7623

For information about the history of the railroad in America

On the Road

Golden Spike National Historic Site

P. O. Box 897

Brigham City, UT 84302

435/471-2209

A national park with walking tours along the Promontory Mountains and driving tours along an original railbed of the transcontinental railroad

INDEX

About the Author

Jean F. Blashfield has worked for publishers in Chicago, Illinois,
and Washington, D.C. A graduate of the University of Michigan,
she has written more than ninety books, most of them for young
people. Jean F. Blashfield has two college-age children and lives
in Delavan, Wisconsin.